Discover the Secrets of the Dark Web

Ethan J. Edwardsf

Stay connected with your business mission; it's the guiding principle.

Stay updated with the evolution of digital wallets; they're centralizing financial transactions and enhancing security.

Stay attentive; noticing the little things shows you care.

Practice appreciation; regularly express gratitude for each other.

Introduction

Welcome to this book, a comprehensive journey into the depths of the internet that few dare to explore. In this guide, we will delve into the hidden corners of cyberspace, shedding light on the history, technologies, myths, and realities of the dark web.

The internet is like an iceberg, with the surface web being the tip visible to all. But what lies below the surface? "What's Below the Surface?" sets the stage for our exploration, introducing you to the intriguing and enigmatic world of the dark web.

To understand the dark web, it's essential to trace its roots, and "The History of the Dark Web, ARPANET and Its Dark Siblings" does just that. We'll delve into the origins of the dark web, its connection to ARPANET, and how it evolved over time.

"The Onion Router" (TOR) is at the heart of the dark web's anonymity, and we'll unravel its inner workings in "The Onion Router." Discover how TOR enables users to navigate the dark web while concealing their identities.

No discussion of the dark web is complete without mentioning "The Silk Road and Other Destinations." We'll take you on a journey to explore the infamous Silk Road and other hidden online destinations, shedding light on both the legitimate and illicit activities that transpire in these digital shadows.

In "A Closer Examination," we'll delve into the shadows of the dark web, separating fact from fiction. Learn about the true nature of the dark web, its uses, and the ethical considerations surrounding its existence.

While the dark web is often associated with illegal activities, "Using TOR Can Help Keep Your Identity Safe" explores how it can be a valuable tool for preserving online privacy and security. Discover how TOR serves as a shield for individuals living under oppressive regimes and the heroes who champion online freedoms.

"The Great Firewall of China" takes us on a journey to a digital society that employs strict censorship and control. Learn how the Chinese government maintains its iron grip on the internet and the tools Chinese citizens use to circumvent these restrictions.

"Myths and Legends Versus Facts" dispels common misconceptions about the dark web. We'll separate fact from fiction and explore what truly thrives in the shadows and what is mere legend.

The dark web is a hub for crypto-commerce, and "Crypto-Commerce" dives into the world of cryptocurrencies and the role they play in underground markets.

"The Threat of Doxing" examines the dangers of having one's personal information exposed online. Discover the dark web's role in both perpetrating and protecting against doxing.

"Creepypasta" takes us into the realm of online horror stories and urban legends. Explore the spine-tingling tales that have originated from the dark web.

"How the Dark Web Saves Lives – Left in the Cold by Big Pharma" sheds light on how the dark web provides a lifeline for individuals in desperate need of medications they cannot obtain through traditional means.

"Stories from the Dark Side" delves into the real-life stories of individuals who have navigated the dark web. These firsthand accounts provide a glimpse into the challenges and rewards of exploring this hidden realm.

"Back to Reality" discusses the implications of dark web exploration on your digital life and online privacy. Learn how to protect yourself when delving into the shadows.

"A Practical Guide to Exploring the Dark Web" provides you with the tools and knowledge needed to embark on your own dark web journey. From the legality of your travels to the essential resources, this section equips you for safe exploration.

As you venture into the depths of the dark web, remember that knowledge is your greatest ally. "TOR Is Looking Out for You (In a Good Way)" explores the measures in place to keep you safe during your digital travels.

Buckle up and prepare to dive into the enigmatic world of the dark web. This book is your passport to understanding, navigating, and demystifying the hidden layers of the internet. Whether you're a curious explorer or a cautious observer, this guide has something to offer as we embark on this digital adventure together.

Contents

CHAPTER 1 WHAT'S BELOW THE SURFACE?

You probably enter the Deep Web every day, without even realizing it.

For decades, the terms "*deep*" and "*dark*" have been used interchangeably (and incorrectly). So much so that *Wired* magazine mentions it in its style guide to ensure writers use the correct terms when reporting on hidden service news. What are hidden services? Unlike human-friendly domain names such as www.amazon.com, a hidden service is comprised of 16 characters followed by the *.onion* domain. This domain will be undetectable by standard search engines but can be found by anyone with Tor software (or other tools) installed on their computer.

In the most basic sense, the **Deep Web** contains content that will not be revealed by a search engine. Just as you can't share a post on Facebook with the world if it's been edited to be viewed by "Friends" only, or a random person cannot access your online bank account (or at least not without a specific skill set), or the public can't view a corporation's private data, the information on the Deep Web not only consists of the majority of the Internet, it is also invisible to most Internet surfers. Even the average online shopping experiences delve into the Deep Web once you begin a detailed search for say, a particular sweater or a pair of shoes. Court records, academic papers, library, and government databases all exist below the surface in the Deep Web.

The iceberg analogy when discussing the regions of the Internet is popular, and for a good reason. The **Surface Web** is that chunk of the Internet visible to the public—or in the case of our iceberg, above water. Like our iceberg, the Surface Web is smaller than what waits for us below. The Surface Web is easily explored via search engines; every site within it is indexed. According to Google, the average search reveals just .03 percent of what the Internet actually contains. The Deep Web in comparison is thousands of times larger.

Although what about the notoriety, the outrageous stories, such as chat rooms where assassins ply their trade, vast illegal drug marketplaces, identify theft, and worse? These do (and do not) occur deeper below the surface of the waves, in something called **The Dark Web**. The Dark Web is a place you'll need specific tools to enter. It exists within the Deep Web, a pocket that grows exponentially each year, and inhabited by not only the curious and the criminal, but by the law enforcement as well.

Why would anyone want to explore the Deep Web or the Dark Web?

There are many benefits to exploring the Internet anonymously. For businesses, this can bring the advantage of gathering knowledge about their customers before their competitors become aware of a trend or consumer chatter. In a quiet, anonymous world that is the Dark Web, consumers don't hold back their opinions, and the corporate world can gain insight it never could on the highly-regulated, even censored Surface Web.

There is a different culture in the Dark Web, however, one that the numbers-obsessed the corporate world might find difficult to parse. The spirit of the Dark Web is that of the *pioneer*, regardless of activity. One story tells of how a Dark Web frequenter purchased a drug of choice from a vendor, only to receive some grams of cane sugar in the mail. When the user told his story in a dark web chatroom, he was contacted by another anonymous entity and found his money refunded, by a seller with a heart of gold who hated to see a dishonorable crime being committed in his corner of the shadownet. Another user found he'd downloaded a Trojan virus that had ridden piggyback atop the bootleg version of *The Sims* PC game he'd purchased; a caring good Samaritan walked him how to rid his computer of it. The Dark Web is a collection of nameless, faceless, and most importantly, *numberless* guests, gathering in the protective darkness of anonymity, for many reasons. For some, however, remaining anonymous is reasonable enough.

What is the structure of the Dark Web and how does it differ from the Internet we use every day? In the most basic sense, the Dark Web operates the same as the Surface Web, in that it speaks the same language. It uses a system of rules, **TCP/IP**, or *Transmission Control Protocol/Internet Protocol*. Using these language rules, one computer may communicate with another computer across the Internet by gathering network packets of data and sending them to the correct place to be received. You've heard of terabytes, gigabytes, megabytes, kilobytes, bytes, and bits—a packet is the smallest unit in this system of measurement. The TCP level of this computer language is responsible for compressing large amounts of data into shareable packets. The IP level is akin to a mile marker, allowing the packets to find their destination across metaphorical miles of the Internet.

TCP/IP started with four distinct layers, the application layer, the transport layer, the internet layer, and the link layer.

The application layer is where the user interacts with the Internet directly via an interface. The transport layer hosts communication between web hosts—either the same host, two different hosts, the local network, or remote networks. The network layer connects those hosts, and the link layer is the physical equipment itself.

After this, the two Webs part ways. Surface web domains are listed with the DNS registry, making them easy to find by traditional web browsers such as Firefox, Chrome, and Safari. Websites on the

Dark Web avoid the DNS registry altogether, and so cannot be accessed by traditional means.

DNS or *Domain Name Servers* are basically your phone books on the Internet. They keep a directory of domain names and convert those into IP addresses, needed by computers who calculate in terms of numeric Internet Protocol addresses rather than catchy website names.

If you want to use the Internet anonymously, it's important to find a reliable DNS provider who won't leak your IP address. Why is this important? Many **ISP** (*Internet Service Providers*) and DNS providers keep logs of your search queries, browsing history, and will even censor what you're able to see. Here are several who do not: FreeDNS and DNS Watch (which not only supports Windows and Mac OS but Linux as well), Cloudflare, Comodo, Level 3, and Verisign, who in the Fall of 2015 announced their new service and the promise that "*Verisign Public DNS is a free DNS service that offers improved DNS stability and security over other alternatives.*"

The user enters a **URL** (*Uniform Resource Locator*) query. That query reaches out to a recursive revolver server, which can be hosted by your Internet Service Provider, your wireless provider, or a third-party provider. The recursive revolver server then finds the correct IP address to match your query—it accomplishes this by connecting with a root server and TLD (top-level domain) server. Verisign currently has access to more root servers than any other DNS. That being said, dark web users are vocal in their mistrust of any company that does not release regular, thorough, and public audits that provide proof of their information gathering (or lack thereof). One company that regularly releases such audits is Cloudflare. Cloudflare also provides an app, called "*1.1.1.1.*" for Android and iOS.

Finally, not only will the right DNS protect your privacy online, it will greatly increase the speed of your browsing, and even provide parental controls in filtering content you'd rather your children not have access to. We'll discuss how to get a DNS up and running on your system later in the book.

In the 1960s, the first message ever to be sent across what would become the Internet was LOG, when a server at MIT crashed and prevented the user from typing LOGIN. Now travelers in the Dark Web, with only their own curiosity to guide them, search for the strange, eerie, and haunting, much like our ancestors wandered into primordial forests seeking adventure.

One user in the Dark Web stumbled upon a vast directory of .html files and images of military and medical faxes. Returning to the top of the sub-directory, the user found a new file had been added, named "Hello There". Clicking that revealed a message "I see you", which prompted the user to immediately get the hell out of Dodge.

But why do we seek out that which might disturb us? Not everything in the Dark Web is as notorious as it's made out to be, but there is plenty there to be found and be shocked by. So why would anyone want to go?

Disgust, as (hopefully) taught to us by our caregivers when we're toddlers, keeps us safe, clean, and out of harm's way. We're taught not to touch something if it might make us sick. And once that set of skills is mastered, we learn to sneak peeks at terrible things for the thrill of it. Those moments of adrenaline hit the same area in the brain—the VTA, or ventral tegmental area—exists within the mesolimbic pathway, and is linked with the neurotransmitter dopamine. In a stressful world, sometimes we look to self-soothe in some incredible ways, and arousal can come from terror, as well as from delight. Experts stress that we haven't gotten worse, as thrill seekers, we've just been given greater access to such thrills, and the Dark Web is a gateway that many say fails to disappoint.

How can we separate the urban legends from the facts when it comes to the Dark Web? One user ironically says, *"The scariest thing about the darknet is the page loading time."* Others claim the truly dark activity is going on right in front of us, so well-encrypted that we'd never know what we're looking at. Truth be told, making money is one of the biggest attractions to the Dark Web. Despite fanciful tales of chatrooms where one can commune with spirits, truer stories involve gambling rings that bet on lower-profile tennis professionals and allow them to earn a considerable living in fixed matches, as well as journalists from oppressed countries using the Dark Web to share information and not risk imprisonment from their governments.

To many, the Dark Web is the last frontier of free speech—*The Uncensored Hidden Wiki* is an example of this, a weighty collection of political rants too extreme for public view. All frontiers have their dangers, due to lack of regulations and the muscle to enforce the law. The same thing that makes the Dark Web so appealing is what makes it so potentially dangerous. Knowing our penchant for shock value, jump scares, and horror, there are those who would peddle such things for a price. Disturbing videos can be unlocked with cryptocurrency, such as that of a pre-teen committing suicide. Rumors abound that identity theft will run you around $850 US. As well as even worse things can be had for free, such as a collection of disturbing videos known simply as *The Gauntlet.* Beyond this, there is no guarantee that a browser such as Tor will totally protect your anonymity; government agencies such as the NSA have been recorded in the process of unburying regular Dark Web users' identities. Regular usage of Tor can actually alert you to the authorities, instead of hiding you from them. In 2014, Comcast service representatives began warning their customers against the use of Tor, claiming it was an illegal web browser. The company then denied the accuracy of these reports in a later statement.

Tor exit nodes are the points from which encrypted Tor data reaches the Internet. Exit nodes are essential to the functionality of Tor, but they can also be abused. One couple—privacy activists from Seattle—was served with a warrant to search their home and hand over the passwords to their computers after monitoring of their exit node linked them to child abuse. Fortunately, nothing illicit was found on the couple's computers and the charges against them were dropped, but they admitted that they were "terrified" and felt "violated" by the experience.

Downloading Tor itself is not illegal nor is the company that updates the software nefarious. Browsing the Dark Web with Tor is also not illegal. Still, how does one explore the Dark Web safely?

Before we learn how to enter the Dark Web, it's best if we learn about its history.

CHAPTER 2 THE HISTORY OF THE DARK WEB, ARPANET AND ITS DARK SIBLINGS

I t was 1969 when that first message sent by the UCLA student Charley Kline across ARPANET set down a metaphorical paving-stone that would one day lead to the infamous "Silk Road", and beyond.

The Advanced Research Projects Agency of the U.S. Defense Department put its money into developing **ARPANET**, or the **Advanced Research Projects Agency Network**, in an effort to create a network using telephone lines that did not utilize a central, hackable core. Though at this time, and at the height of the Cold War, no one could yet imagine an enemy taking over and controlling a network—they were merely afraid of a major communications blackout. The research had a decidedly academic intent but used current politics to give its work greater emphasis. As the work continued, the network grew tremendously, much to the satisfaction of the Defense Department, and became very much like what the Internet looks like today, albeit smaller.

A decade earlier, a 61-billion-dollar project called SAGE (*Semi-Automatic Ground Environment*) had been launched to determine enemy aircraft from our own. 24 hours a day, 7 days a week, the SAGE network scanned the skies for Soviet planes carrying nuclear weapons. At the NORAD headquarters (*North American Aerospace Defense Command*) on Cheyenne Mountain, SAGE even provided an enormous "war room" styled map of North America. The SAGE network was comprised of twenty-three massive, main-frame computers—the AN/FSQ7 built by IBM, each weighing 250 tons, occupying a half-acre of space, containing 60,000 vacuum tubes and 49,000 electron tubes. Each of these computers was placed at a radar-station housed within a windowless, four-story concrete building, where the information gathered was processed by human technicians in real time by using machines with magnetic-core memory. (*image above*)

As the technician sat at their post, they would watch a screen for incoming "blips", and tap each blip with a light-pen, thus alerting the computer to monitor that aircraft carefully.

In hindsight, SAGE did very little to protect against Soviet planes. If one plane jammed the signal, the entire system would malfunction. Luckily for us, the technology gave way to better things, such as the Internet as we now know it.

ARPA was eventually demilitarized when revolutionary thinker and scientist Joseph Carl Robnett Licklider—or "*Lick*" as he preferred to be called—joined ARPA'S Information Processing Techniques Office or IPTO. The recipient of a doctorate from the University of Rochester and frequent Harvard lecturer, his vision of a future where humans and computers worked in tandem to create a better world provided fertile intellectual ground for the now liberated project. That is how in the wake of former military conservatism, ARPA became the gateway to now-modern concepts of computer flight simulation, multiprogramming, and computer graphics. Four years later, Licklider was replaced by Robert Taylor as director. Taylor observed technicians communicating with each other over teletype machines that were hooked up to the mainframe computers. Taylor realized the waste and unnecessary cost of using teletype machines when a single language could be created to allow the computers to speak directly to each other over a network, and his proposal for the funding for ARPANET was born. In an essay that "Lick" and Taylor co-wrote, this statement augured the future of the modern Internet and social media: "*In a few years, men will be able to communicate more effectively through a machine than face to face.*"

The next breakthrough occurred from the desire to move beyond using dedicated, analog circuitry (used by telephones) that remained "on" once activated. Packet switching (at first called "hot potato routing") was introduced as a digital solution to this problem. With digital communication between computers became error-free, with no need for conversion or risk of transformation error. The redundancy created by using packet switches also meant that if one link was damaged, the rest of the network of links would survive. In time, telecommunications companies came to trust a packet switching network as a more efficient, faster means of sharing information.

But what actually is "*packet-switching*"? Take a standard email for instance. Via packet-switching, the email is broken into smaller pieces of information, then sent across a network. Each piece travels along a different route, at a different pace, and not necessarily in order—but when all of the pieces arrive at the receiving end they are precisely reassembled as per each packet's "*header*", which contains instructions as to where it should be placed in the sum total. Data coursing over telephone lines will follow the path of least resistance and prevent an overload of activity.

When ARPANET was in its infancy, only three tasks could be performed: logging into the system itself, printing to a remote printer, or sharing files between computers. By the late '60s, however, the interest in the project was so great that colleges across the US were jockeying for a position to connect to ARPANET, and thus began a period of intense growth. April 1971 saw 15 nodes and 23 terminals added to the network. NASA, MIT, BBN, and Rand joined the network as well. By early 1973, the network had 20 more connected nodes, and by 1976, a total of 63 connected nodes. In 1971, contractor BBN's Ray Tomlinson wrote the first ever email program. The first email ever sent was a random tapping of keys, akin to "QWERTYUIOP". Soon, email mailing lists gave way to virtual discussion groups, and the term "LISTSERVs" was coined.

So how did we get from this basic, primitive, and relatively wholesome beginning to the Dark Web?

As it turns out, the Dark Web was there all along.

Coinciding with ARPANET, small networks are known as *darknets* appeared. They were capable of receiving data from other computers on ARPANET but were undetectable by those computers. Their addresses were secret, and they could not receive an Internet Control Message Protocol (ICMP), or ping, nor would they reply to inquiries. Primarily used for file sharing, these darknets prove that the need for anonymity is not new, nor is it modern.

THE ONION ROUTER

There's a feud happening silently every day that you and I are unaware of. The Navy—who developed the Tor browser, infuriates the Army, or more specifically the NSA, who are constantly trying to figure out how to snoop around Tor. Both are headquartered in Maryland, mere miles from each other.

The part of the federal US government that's in charge of propaganda is called BBG, or the *Broadcasting Board of Governors (as of 2018 - U.S. Agency for Global Media (USAGM))*, and it funds Tor to this day. Coupled with funding coming directly from the State Department, Tor and the Navy can't lose, though it's the NSA's job to keep trying to break it.

Paul Syverson, David Goldschlag, and Michael Reed developed the idea of "onion routing" in the '90s at the US Naval Research Laboratory. Roger Dingledine and Nick Mathewson perfected the concept, and the TOR Project was officially launched on September

20th, 2002. The Electronic Frontier Foundation, or EFF, continued its funding to further develop the project.

Tor was developed to protect the identities of military personnel stationed overseas, and in an effort to further mask these troops' identities and locations, Tor was released to the public in October 2003 as a free, open-source browser, with the aim of hiding military personnel amid the traffic of anonymous civilian users.

The Tor Project itself is a non-profit organization that keeps Tor's updates current. Additional financial assistance is provided by individual sponsors and even the country of Sweden.

How Tor works is pretty simple.

Tor itself is a network, which is populated by thousands of volunteer routers, also known as nodes. A user's data is encrypted at least three different points, or relays, before reaching its destination. This is also what makes it difficult (and in most hands, impossible) to trace the user or client. Their address and identity are masked in triplicate. Tor not only hides identities of individual users but entire websites also, and helps with the configuration of Peer to Peer (P2P) applications that allow users to share and download torrent files.

When I wrote this, there were 6,483 exit nodes and nearly 7,000 total relays, with nearly 3,000 bridges running. There are three different types of nodes you can run if you'd like to volunteer on Tor: middle relays, exit relays, and bridges. Middle relays pass the data along and maintain its speed while encrypting it, and a Tor user can easily find a middle relay to connect to. It's pretty safe to connect to a middle relay as well since its location is hidden. Exit relays are the last stop on the encryption road, and viewable to everyone on the network. If an unsavory user does something illegal on the network, the exit relay may take the fall for it. Exit relays are definitely not for the hobbyist or someone using their personal computer in their home. Police may seize your computer if someone compromises your relay to engage in illegal activity. Bridge relays on the Tor network are not publicly listed and help in avoiding censorship in countries such as in China. Like middle relays, bridges are also considered safe to run in your home.

According to the EFF (*Electronic Frontier Foundation*), no one has ever been prosecuted in the US for running a Tor relay, and that running a relay is itself a legal act. That being said, using Tor for illegal activities is, of course, illegal. Using it for freedom of speech, to avoid censorship, to support human rights, and to maintain anonymity—all perfectly legal and in the spirit which Tor continues to thrive today.

Another topic of interest here: you may run the risk of getting a DMCA complaint from your Internet service provider. The *Digital Millennium Copyright Act* protects copyrighted material from being transmitted illegally over the Internet. On the Tor project website, you'll find a template for you to use in order to respond to such a complaint: https://2019.www.torproject.org/eff/tor-dmca-response.html.en

Also, be prepared to constantly see your IP address announced to you if you go seeking a hidden service browser to install. It's startling at first, but you'll get used to it.

So, is Tor the Dark Web and Dark Web Tor? Absolutely not. Tor is only *one* network that exists in the Dark Web. There are others, such as Hornet, Freenet, and I2P, which we'll discuss later on in the book.

THE SILK ROAD AND OTHER DESTINATIONS

Ross William Ulbricht, who called himself *"The Dread Pirate Roberts"*, claimed he would never be arrested.

With the FBI takedown of 29-year-old Ulbricht, the Silk Road's biggest drug dealer, the notorious Silk Road website came to an end. Ulbricht was charged with money laundering, narcotics traffic conspiracy, as well as computer hacking (*unauthorized access into someone else's computer*). The US Department of Justice seized Silk Road's website, nearly $4 billion dollars in bitcoins (*the main currency of the Dark Web*), and halted what was thought to be nearly $40 million in annual revenue. That figure may be astoundingly more but was not proven. Internet chatter claims Ulbricht had the audacity to give a Forbes' interview, and that at that point everyone could see the end for him was nigh. Journalist Adrian

Chen's 2011 Gawker article covering the Silk Road could not have helped Ulbricht's cause either.

The Silk Road lasted two and a half years. Still, how did it, and other points of interest in the Tor network, begin?

In 2011, Ulbricht reached out anonymously for feedback to an idea of his. In a message board of the website Shroomery.org, he asked:

"I came across this website called Silk Road. It's a Tor hidden service that claims to allow you to buy and sell anything online anonymously. I'm thinking of buying off it, but I wanted to see if anyone here had heard of it and would recommend it.

I found it through silkroad420.wordpress.com, which, if you have a tor browser, directs you to the real site at http://tydgccykixpbu6uz.onion.

Let me know what you think..."

Just in case that tactic didn't work, Ulbricht also posted on a Bitcoin forum a couple of days later, and sparked instant excitement there.

Ulbricht's great idea thrived, created a boom in Bitcoin, but ultimately fell because of its originator's ego. Ulbricht's boasts and sloppy tactics cost him his privacy, and eventually, his freedom.

A second Silk Road website attempted to take the original's place— it lasted a year and a day. Successors such as *AlphaBay*—believed to have been the largest online drug marketplace in the world, and

Hansa – were shut down in 2017 after an international coordinated effort by law enforcement infiltrated the sites.

A more successful pharmaceutical marketplace, the Russian hidden service site *RAMP*, continues to do business today, but fortunately for you, it's conducted entirely in Russian. (And even if you speak fluent Russian, I'd advise you not to go there).

By now you might be asking—so where *can* I go? What's in it for me? Should I even bother exploring the Tor network?

ProPublica, an independent, US non-profit newsroom based in New York City, is not only the recipient of the Pulitzer Prize for investigative journalism but also has a "*.onion*" address. Facebook has a Tor address too, but we likely don't need to mention the weirdness of such a privacy-invasive company existing in the anonymity of the Dark Web.

Skipping right along—*Sci-Hub*, heroes to some, villains to others, gives access to over 50 million pages of scientific research to those who would not normally be able to afford such knowledge. Research papers typically exist behind paywalls, and Sci-Hub gains access to these papers via leaked credentials, then turns around hosts the captured work for any visitor to explore.

Another useful site, *DuckDuckGo*, is the Dark Web's alternative to Google, for those who prefer to retain their anonymity while searching the web. DuckDuckGo is incredibly fast and reliable, and above all, safe.

Tor Mail existed for a while as the Dark Web's email service but was taken down after an investigation into illegal activity. Mail2Tor seems to have risen as its feisty replacement and states with a message on its Surface Web website that, "*None of the Mail2Tor mail systems are hosted on this server, or on any server that you can find the IP address. Seizing or shutting down this website will have no effect on us.*"

The Hub is an independent Dark Web forum that is home to the passionate harm-reduction community, giving free advice to those who might self-medicate and how to do so safely, if possible. Finally, the world's most popular Bitcoin wallet, called Blockchain, is available with a .onion address.

As the last point, there is the matter of the *Hidden Wiki*, the Tor network's infamous guide to all of the other sites on the network. It's a matter of debate as to whether or not the Hidden Wiki is safe to explore. There are certainly legal, legitimate sites the links of which can be found in the Wiki, but because it is a Wiki and publicly-editable page, anyone can go in and tamper with a link to redirect you to an unsavory destination. As a rule, anything asking you to spend your money should be avoided, as well as anything even remotely hinting at the terrible subject of "CP" (i.e. child pornography). A breakthrough occurred in March of 2014, when a Dark Web persona named "*Intangir*" hacked the Hidden Wiki and deleted all of the CP links, despite mixed responses of praise and derision that he'd censored what should remain uncensored. Four years later, the Hidden Wiki remains a place in which to tread carefully, though it contains many links that are completely safe and thankfully, their descriptions will let you know well before you journey to them.

There are now many wikis designed to point you to the various sites of the onion network. One user swears by the method of avoiding any site that starts with a plethora of 1's and A's.

CHAPTER 3 A CLOSER EXAM NAT ON

SHADOWS IN THE DARKNESS

So, who actually uses the Dark Web? Criminals? Hackers and porn peddlers? The answer to that is yes, and also no.

Fernando Caudevilla, also known in the hidden services community as *Doctor X*, is a primary care physician in Madrid, and also frequents the Dark Web to answer visitors' questions about harm reduction. Because of the difficulty drug users face in getting medical advice, Caudevilla finds himself more approachable in an anonymous setting, kind of like a Dark Web outreach, although he prefers the term "*Deep Web*" and its neutrality, even though the Dark Web is a part of the Deep Web, being contained by it.

Despite all the negative connotations drug dealers and drug users shoulder (they are, after all, violating the law), Caudevilla observes a great amount of trust and honor in cryptocurrency markets of the Dark Web. Buyers will put their money in escrow, deliverable to the seller once the product is received. According to Caudevilla, this practice has made cryptocurrency markets wildly successful. In addition, Caudevilla is a type of advocate for drug users, citing their civil and human rights, rights to health care and treatment. In Russia, for instance, drug addicts are treated harshly and given no access to treatment to help them gain sobriety. Methadone clinics do not exist. In a cryptocurrency darknet market, they might actually find the means with which to quit a very dangerous drug, and Caudevilla has advised many overseas methadone users how to taper their daily dose so as not to relapse and end up back where they'd started.

His unconditional advice and refusal to judge those seeking it has made Doctor X one of the most respected men of the Dark Web. He does not advise everyone equally, however. "If I talked to a classroom of 15-year-olds I would not advise them to use cocaine," he said in a 2014 Sydney-based article.

Who else uses the Dark Web? Surprisingly, more and more parents.

In November of 2014, a 12-year-old girl living outside of Baltimore left home one morning for school. Four days later, found by North Carolina law enforcement with the assistance of the FBI, the girl was found and brought home, but she told a blood-chilling story of how her abductor had "non-consensual sex with her".

Was this just a random abduction? No. Microsoft provided transcripts of the girl's *Xbox Live* chats with her would-be abductor where he manipulated her into thinking he was safe to meet, nearly a month before he intercepted her trip to school in his truck. They'd also been communicating via *Kik*, a messenger app she'd been told by her parents she was not allowed to install. Luckily, she was found before the situation could escalate from the terrible to the unthinkable.

But what about children who don't chat online? Are they safe?

Not necessarily. A parent browsing the Surface Web without a **VPN** (*virtual private network*, which we'll discuss later in the book), is giving their IP address to any who would look for it. With an IP address, someone can type it into the website http://whois.domaintools.com/{IPADDRESS} and get the user's proximity, their country of origin, and their Internet Service Provider. Then, the searcher can call the ISP and perhaps wrangle a physical address from them, or in a more devious way, get the user's email address and phish for the physical address. There are even websites, like *iplocation.net* or *whatismyipaddress.com*, that will narrow down an address from an IP address.

How to prevent a would-be predator from finding your house and potentially harming your family or property? Beyond monitoring what your children do online and who they communicate with, use a browser such as Tor, and use a Virtual Private Network while doing so.

USING TOR CAN HELP KEEP YOUR IDENTITY SAFE

A recent, disturbing version of identity theft is medical identity theft. Thieves use stolen identities for their hospital bills, to fill prescriptions, and get services on your medical insurance's coverage. Health insurance companies and hospital databases have been hacked to reveal the identities of their patients, but what can you do from home to protect your identity from being compromised? Even Forbes Magazine recommends using Tor to protect privacy.

HEROES OF THE DARK WEB

Activism, journalism, and science. What keeps our world safe, our freedom intact, and our health in the forefront of public concern? In April 2018, dozens of US news anchors were recorded reading the exact same speech—a speech they'd been ordered to recite by Sinclair Broadcasting Group. The speech spouted propaganda about "*fake news*" and "*one-sided journalism*", and seemed to be mimicking the talking points of the American president Donald Trump. If maintaining integrity in American journalism is difficult, imagine in other countries, such as China, Uganda, and Brazil?

Those countries were ranked 176th, 117th, and 102nd by Reporters Without Borders' 2018 World Press Freedom Index. The United States was ranked 45th.

The Tor project is involved with *SecureDrop*, an open-source system for documents to be anonymously submitted. SecureDrop was designed by the late activist and programmer Aaron Swartz, who co-founded Reddit and who committed suicide when faced with a 35-year long prison sentence after allegedly downloading millions of journal articles from the JSTOR database on the MIT campus. It is believed that Aaron died fighting to free publicly-funded scientific literature that would be kept from the very researchers who published it (and who could not afford to access it).

Alexandra Elbakyan, a Kazakhstani graduate student who founded Sci-Hub, also works to make scientific journals available to the students who can't afford them. Where a year's subscription to a chemistry journal can cost a whopping $4,773 US, and a subscription and even to a general science journal can cost $1,556 US per year, a few can afford to further themselves without inside access to an institution of higher learning, and even colleges are struggling to afford the prices. While Elbakyan and Swartz are very different people with different backgrounds, perhaps at one time, their goals were the same.

SecureDrop's co-creator James Dolan, a marine who served in the Iraq War and who was believed to have suffered from PTSD, also took his life, after first seeing SecureDrop's implementation through to where it was stable enough to be picked up and funded by FPF, or the Freedom of the Press Foundation. SecureDrop is a lifeline to journalists who would face imprisonment or death in the repressive nations in which they operate. The CPJ, or Committee to Protect Journalists, utilizes SecureDrop to better enable journalists, whistleblowers, and activists. Currently, major news organizations such as The Associated Press, The New York Times, The Washington Post, The CBC, Dagbladet, and ProPublica also use SecureDrop.

Law enforcement also uses the Dark Web and with great effectiveness. While hidden service sites have the unsavory reputation of being lawless lands where murder-for-hire is advertised and child abuse being promoted, law enforcement agents are actually helping steer what already is (and could be even more in the future) an important territory for free speech and civil liberties away from those who would do harm to their fellow citizens. Using a technique frequently used by hackers, FBI agents install malware that downloads onto computers accessing illegal sites, such as *Playpen*, and force these computers to reveal their actual address. With a second warrant, agents are able to arrest these users in their homes and stop them from contributing to the very real problem of human trafficking and child pornography. In the case of Playpen, the FBI's warrant allowed them to harvest the IP addresses of 1,300 computers, resulting in the arrest of 137 people. As for Playpen, the site was seized by the FBI and was shut down.

Environmental groups are increasingly coming under surveillance in the US, under post-911 legislation. Congressmen Rob Bishop of Utah and Bruce Westerman of Arkansas gave WRI (*World Resources Unit*) an ultimatum to produce documents of their work in China and asked if anyone in their organization had registered as a foreign agent. WRI is well respected across the world as an international climate and environmental research group, and it reiterated its purpose and goals when asked about the accusatory letter sent to them. In addition to WRI, the Center for Biological Diversity, and the National Resources Defense Council came under Congressman Bishop's scrutiny for their work overseas. These organizations returned fire, metaphorically, when they stated that they're under no obligation to register as foreign agents when they do not work at the behest of the countries in which they're doing research (in this case, China and Japan).

Many believe these groups were targeted because of a current negative light China's relation exists in, regarding US foreign policy. In reality, the groups insist it is a smokescreen to cover up the attempted silencing of groups critical of the US federal governments attack the environment, and that it harkens back to the Cold War when the US government was accused of "red-baiting".

On the Tor project website, stories of people around the world using Tor for good are shared. One such story of an environmental activist and journalist named Jon talks about his work in Uganda (ranked 117th in the World Press Freedom Chart, if you recall). Jon lives in Hoima, an oil city, and uses Tor to anonymously publish his blog. Local police in Hoima frequently seize privately-owned electronic equipment, forcing journalists to declassify their sources.

Back in the US, small-town activists are using the Dark Web to share information in an attempt to free their communities from strangleholds by big corporations taking advantage of the town's small government and law enforcement. One anonymous woman said her work if discovered, could lead to harm or fatal accidents.

Tor can also help employees circumvent blocked information by the companies or unions they work for. And many companies do retaliate - a Canadian Internet Service Provider cut off access to its employees' own union website.

THE GREAT FIREWALL OF CHINA

China tops Iran as the worst for online censorship. The news website ProPublica chose to move its content to a *.onion* site on the Tor network after their own project, an interactive program called "Inside the Firewall", inspired them to act regarding their own security and freedom of speech. The app revealed to them China's practicing of tracking and censoring other countries' news sites within their borders. ProPublica's Edwin Torres decided to see what would happen if he used some ProPublica-related content on the Tor network, in an effort to see if a viewer from a content-restricted country such as China could actually have access to it, prompting the website to create the Tor-based sister location. The *.onion* site for ProPublica is located at *propub3r6espa33w.onion*

In December of 2015, the Chinese president gave a speech at China's second annual World Internet Conference. The message was respectful regarding other nations' use of the Internet, but it carried a warning towards the citizens of China, and it continued the president's agenda of the Chinese Internet being a quarantined space, heavily censored and watched for anti-state activity. The Chinese blog host, Sina Weibo, its interface similar to that of Twitter's, had become a ghost town under the new, stricter government policies.

Before Xi Jinping came to the mantle of China's highest office in 2012, the Chinese Internet was markedly different. Bloggers had millions of followers and spoke their minds about political happenings. Virtual Private Networks helped users access hidden sites, and astoundingly, citizens networked to whistle blow the corrupt actions of authorities. Though the fear of being doxed or arrested was growing in the shadows of the days to come.

Once Xi Jinping came into power, however, everything changed. The Chinese president holds that a citizen of the republic must not have a second self, or persona—being online is no exception. They must uphold the values of the Chinese government at all times. There is no room for criticism or analysis; they simply do not possess the right to such things.

Try to imagine what it would be like to live according to *those* standards.

Xi Jinping's technological spearhead to invest in ways and means to monitor his country's online activity is tremendous. Beyond being able to keep tabs on its citizens, the censorship efforts mean foreign countries are at a grave disadvantage to doing business on Chinese soil—virtual or otherwise. Often citing a sovereign right to control China's Internet, Xi Jinping begins to sound as arrogant and out of touch with reality as his neighbor, Kim Jong-un.

The developer credited for laying the foundation for what is now known as the *Great Firewall of China* is Fang Binxing. After intensive funding and support from the Chinese government in the early 2000s, Fang was instrumental in helping Beijing block Google for the first time in China's history. Two years later, Google would hobble out a censored version of itself for China's use.

In 2004, in an eerie similarity to the Russian bots who would come to plague the US' social media forums during the 2016 presidential election, Chinese universities recruited students to go online and steer conversations revolving (delicately) around political themes to favor the Chinese government. They would also report any illegal comments. The students were reported to be paid a miserly fifty cents per post.

Such repression always and inevitably leads to pushback. The *Human Flesh Search Engine* rose to popularity after a young woman who was raped received no justice (she was committed to an institution after telling the authorities of her plight), and a blogger brought her story to public light. The Human Flesh Search Engine is a phenomenon where Internet users band together to track down and seek justice for criminals, vigilante-style. It survives today, even having (wrongfully) exacted its punishment in 2017 for a police officer who mortally wounded a golden retriever. After further investigation, it turns out the police officer was mistaken for the dog's actual abuser in a poor quality video of the attack.

The Search Engine came into existence in 2001 on China's popular forum MOP, and while it rose to popularity because of a need for Chinese citizens to network without the dangerous and self-damning process of using a search engine on such a thoroughly monitored Chinese Internet (instead they network with each other on personal websites and forums), it is now more frequently a series of public witch hunts resulting in doxing and seeking vigilante justice upon the wrong, innocent citizen. If found to be engaging in the practice of Human Flesh searches (not searching for human flesh, mind you—just literally going person to person online for information), the penalty is now severe: a 7-year prison term. Despite the potential consequences—and public criticism of the practice in light of the wrong people being targeted even threatened with physical injury and death—the Human Flesh Search Engine is as popular as ever.

One of Xi Jinping's speeches was leaked to the public in 2013, and in that, he revealed his vision as the Internet is a place of battle. The Chinese government's weapon of choice? Artfully constructed propaganda, including a music video instructing the viewers on how to properly speak to their leader.

In 2015, most of the Virtual Private Networks Chinese citizens had faithfully used to get around their government's restrictive practices in the Great Firewall were thwarted, even though the VPNs had become an integral part of both online business and commerce. The Great Cannon was introduced onto the online battlefield, using the Internet user's activities against them by capturing and rewriting online content. The Chinese search engine *Baidu* found its customers hacked during one of the first DDoS (*Distributed Denial of Service*) attacks of the Great Cannon. The New York Times' Chinese mirror site and the *GreatFire.org*, an anti-censorship movement site, were also attacked.

Another perhaps more insidious method of the Chinese government to control and punish illegal online content is to restrict Internet-based rumors. A Chinese court ruled that if a web author's content contained lies or rumors against the republic and was either shared five hundred times or seen by 5,000 viewers, the author could face three years in prison.

This practice seems particularly cruel when we stop to think about how essential and vital an active, online community is during times of national crisis. When huge flooding in the Hebei province prompted people to go online in search of news of their loved ones, the Great Firewall cracked down on reports of the deaths, accusing those trying to post current information as spreading rumors and false news.

Today, the Great Firewall of China renders forbidden content either invisible to the user or excruciatingly slow to load. Few citizens even try to scale the Wall, having had to submit to existing within the small, virtual plot their government has allotted to them. Chinese scholars and scientists have to work within this blockaded vacuum of an Internet, cut off completely from the wealth of information the rest of the world offers. In addition to China's restrictive practices hurting its students, researches, and developers, its censorship stands to backfire against its goals to become a force to reckon with in international markets. Its iron grip on the flow of online information is also its Achilles Heel.

The effects of The Great Firewall and Great Cannon have also contributed to a noticeable *brain drain* of Chinese students who go to study abroad, but choose to not return due to the restrictions they'll face on home soil. Thus, China loses highly skilled labor yearly, another conflict with its agenda for international business success.

In 2012, China's Great Firewall was able to detect the Tor network because of the unusual and distinct pattern of data flow along the network's nodes and relays. To this day, China—along with Russia and Argentina—is proving to continue to be successful in blocking those who would use Tor.

LIFE IN A DIGITAL SOCIETY

How free is our freedom of speech? Stories of employees being fired after posting their thoughts or feelings of the companies they work for are abundant. In most US states, employees are at their workplace "at will", meaning they can be fired for any reason or no reason at all. The First Amendment does not protect the worker in the workplace. There's even a term, "*Dooced*", coined after a woman named Heather B. Armstrong was fired from her job after she was discovered to be the author of the popular blog "Dooce".

So how to share personal insights about your life, via a blog, without outing yourself and risking being let go at work? Bloggers have also been targeted for writing about unpopular opinions, standing up for the rights of women, minorities, and other marginalized groups. When your freedom of speech comes at a cost of your life, what can you do?

Using encryption software that can either render your email address anonymously temporarily or every time you log in, such as *MintEmail*, *RiseUp*, and *Hushmail*. Remember—whenever you are using services such as these, you are diving beneath the Surface Web and populating the Deep Web. Masking your IP address during your entire blogging sessions can be accomplished by using, of course, Tor, but it can also be accomplished by using an anonymous proxy server (for instance, *hide.me*).

While nothing guarantees a blogger's absolute anonymity (especially if the blogger uses a Google-based platform, Google has been pressured to reveal the identity of some of its users in the courtroom), and even Matt Zimmerman (senior staff attorney at the Electronic Frontier Foundation and not to be confused with the founder of Facebook) says that no tool utilized to mask a person's online identity is <u>100% effective</u>, therefore going Deep before you publish your thoughts might be a worthy practice to consider.

CHAPTER 4 MYTHS AND LEGENDS VERSUS FACTS

WHAT THRIVES IN THE SHADOWS (AND WHAT SIMPLY PRETENDS TO)

It is believed that underground markets first took root in *Internet Relay Chatrooms* or IRC. IRC was invented by a Finnish grad student, Jarkko Oikarinen. IRC is most famous for the Iraqi invasion of Kuwait in 1991 when users logged in to get real-time updates of the event via an IRC link that managed to keep functioning a week after radio and television broadcasts went dead.

Still, where are the underground markets now? Some boldly sell their wares in plain sight on the Surface Web, but most choose to operate in the relative darkness of the Deep Web. One advertisement (on a page about darknet storefronts, on the Surface Web, hilariously) reads: *"Dream Market {dark-web-URL} - Drugs, Digital Goods, Hacking, Fraud, Counterfeit, Electronic, Defense, Jewelry, Software, Erotica, Data Leaks, and so on!"*

Smart chips got added to our credit and debit cards in part to prevent the phenomenon of *"cloning"* credit cards—though if you order a third-party debit card such as Netspend Western Union prepaid, you'll find it's missing a chip. In the Dark Web, cloned cards can be purchased from such comically normal-sounding storefronts as *"A-1 Quality Credit Cards"* and *"Dreamweaver"*. Some sites can clone cards with chips, others promise realistic and instantly-usable like Amazon, Walmart, Apple, or eBay gift cards, and others require that you use their card tutorials (which you also have to pay for). The cards come with readily-loaded and an agreed upon balance.

Another site sells cloned PayPal accounts, and still, another offers a Litecoin (another cryptocurrency like Bitcoin) wallet service. One site called unremarkably "WeBuyBitcoins", will purchase your Bitcoin balance for cash. Counterfeit money in a variety of non-crypto currencies, fake Western Union transfers, whatever can be imagined can usually be found, though purchase at your own peril (because it's all highly illegal of course) At best, you can lose your money—at worst, your freedom.

The Dark Web also hosts a plethora of "*hitman for hire*" sites. The validity of these is a popular topic for debate, and I wouldn't recommend you go poking around for them. In the off-chance that you might stumble upon a site that's real, chances are that a law enforcement agent has, too. Not the folks you want to be rubbing shoulders with, all around.

Gambling and gaming sites can be found as well. From a site as innocuous as *TheChess* (wherein all sincerity you can play and talk about chess) to *Xmatches* (fixed football matches), casino gambling sites, and even a site called *Onion Lotto*—you'll need to spend at least .0002 BTC to get the chance of winning 99.9% of the total collected from the other players in the game.

Dark Web forum sites such as *Leaked Forums*, *Exploit.in*, *Lampeduza*, *Sky-fraud*, and *HackerForums* offer things such as escrow services, hosting services, personal identification information, credit card information, black hat search engine optimization, malware software kits, stolen credentials such as social media accounts, serial keys for commercial software such as Microsoft Office and antivirus protection, DDoS attacks*, and *crypters* (tools that can manipulate malware can make it harder to detect by security software. These forums often vet new members, meaning you can't join them unless a member knows you and can recommend you. Other forums require payment to join.

__DDoS__, or distributed denial of service, is an attack in which multiple compromised computer systems attack a target (such as a server or a website) and cause a denial of service for users of that site.

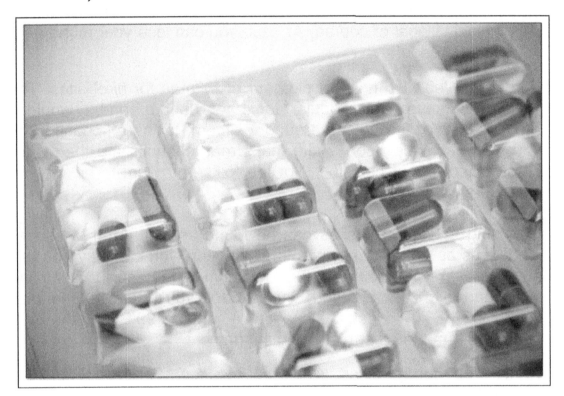

CRYPTO-COMMERCE

If you're going to want to do a business of any kind in the Dark Web, you'll need an amount of cryptocurrency. Here is where we introduce Satoshi Nakamoto.

It's not known if this is a person, people, or an organization, but Satoshi Nakamoto is behind the invention of Bitcoin. There is a profile for the name that would lead us to believe Nakamoto is a 54-

year-old man living in Japan. Regardless, Nakamoto's legacy changed the world, and the face of commerce; the current worth of Bitcoin currency is believed to be over $100 billion USD. Part of the success of Bitcoin was the development of blockchain technology.

A *blockchain* is in a sense a continuously updated database that, instead of being kept in a single, central location, is shared by multiple users, all receiving the updates together. Thus, a blockchain's information is available to anyone and kept in the public eye. Unlike traditional online banking transactions where only one party can alter the information at a time, a blockchain is kept accessible to all parties, rather like a Google Docs document. Having identical, multiple versions of the blockchain data prevents anyone from bringing down the network by targeting one node. In addition, because everything is transparent, and a group effort, accountability is not an issue. Financial experts believe blockchain technology to be the next huge trend in traditional banking; each customer owns their own data because it's kept constantly available to them.

All Bitcoin transactions are recorded and available for public view via the blockchain database. This would give anyone some pause, however—if the whole point of using the Dark/Deep Web is to protect one's identity, then why would cryptocurrency which utilizes blockchain technology be desirable? It's desirable because of its robust, incorruptible structure, but we can use it and still maintain our anonymity. The way to accomplish this? *Bitcoin tumblers.* Remember when we discussed data packets—how your simple email became fragmented into different parts only to be reassembled at the receiving end? A Bitcoin tumbler or mixer is somewhat like that. Your Bitcoins—digital currency comprised of data—get broken into pieces, and mixed with another customer's pieces. This sounds complicated, but it's actually pretty simple to accomplish.

A third-party known as a Bitcoin tumbler will provide the service of mixing your coins and breaking the visible chain between your online wallet and your coins' destination. You can use a service such as *Cloakcoin*, who will take care of masking your transactions with their open-source software solutions, such as *Enigma*, a volunteer network based on customers willing to allow Cloakcoin to use their online wallets as temporary stopping points for another customers' currency. The volunteers are rewarded for their service with a 6% annual interest rate.

It's good practice for all users of cryptocurrency to use a Bitcoin tumbler, but for those who seek Dark Web markets, it would be foolish not to take avail of them. To get started, you need the Tor browser, a stash of Bitcoins, and a wallet in which to keep them. What is a *Bitcoin wallet*? A wallet is a collection of Bitcoin addresses and private keys. What is a *Bitcoin address*? The address is a string of 34 numbers and letters, known together as a cryptographic hash, while a private key has 64 numbers and letters and is the proof, the "title" that you own that address. Each time you go online to conduct a transaction, you will receive a new address to use in that transaction, similar to a code being sent to your phone for identity verification when you log into a traditional, online bank account. Bitcoin miners (who volunteer to maintain the network) receive the transaction and confirm it, and the seller successfully receives your currency.

Create three, separate wallets and move your BTC from the first to the second, using a Bitcoin tumbler service, and then move them to the third. Make sure to avoid any Dark Web markets that insist you have JavaScript enabled; that is a red flag for trouble. Once the tumbler service has completed its task, you can restart your browser and go ahead with your purchase. *Chipmixer* is one tumbler with a good reputation. Some others are *BestMixer*, *BitBlender*, and *BitCloak*.

Another method is to change your cryptocurrency completely, then change it back. According to The Motley Fool, there are currently 1,658 cryptocurrencies. The most popular of these is, of course, *Bitcoin*, followed by *Ethereum*, *Ripple*, *Litecoin*, *EOS*, *Stellar* etc. There is even *Dogecoin* if you fancy the name (try not to laugh when you imagine a Shiba Inu conducting your transactions). A service such as *Changelly* or *Shapeshift* can exchange your online currencies for you.

THE THREAT OF DOXING

Doxing (or **doxxing**) is an abbreviation of "*dropping documents*". It is used to target people—often wrongly—by exposing their real-life identities after an online observer deems them guilty of some offense. Anything from personal financial records, addresses of beloved family members, medical records, and be dumped online for the public to see, and frighteningly, act upon. Even more terrifying is the fact that doxing is not prosecutable under the law unless it's part of a greater campaign of harassment. One tactic of *doxxers*, called swatting, can result in loss of life—it's where the local police or SWAT team are called to an innocent person's home.

Assuming you want to continue to sleep well at night, the question arises—how can we prevent being doxed? Many of us leave key details about our private life on the Surface Web whenever we visit there. Especially with the popularity of social media, we may be coaxed to reveal way too much of our identities, including location, loved ones, and workplace, in an effort to connect with others and make ourselves accessible. Such accessibility comes with a price. Arguing on message boards and in online forums can make one a target for doxing or swatting. Two rivals playing *Call of Duty* online resulted in one swatting the other, and when the police arrived at the victim's home, they fatally shot him.

A hacker can utilize a technique called "*packet sniffing*" to intercept, break down, and analyze the data that you send via a Wi-Fi network. Remember data packets? A packet sniffer is very much like a would-be burglar rifling through your trash to find personal information you naively chose not to shred.

In the story of Dread Pirate Roberts/Ross Ulbricht, the mastermind behind Silk Road, authorities linked information they obtained through Ulbricht's online boasts and statements. The loudest voice attracts the most attention.

Documents you post online contain "metadata". If you right-click on one of your documents, you might be surprised at what is stored there about you. Another technique of hackers is to email or message their victim with a string of code that reveals the receiver's IP address when the letter or private message is opened.

Again, using a Virtual Private Network is essential to protecting yourself whenever you're online. Another tip from the experts—*never* use a social media website to login or register with a new site or service. Using Facebook to sign up for something shares way too much of your information. Just because it's easier, doesn't mean it's better. Also considering installing Tor on your cell phone. In order to do so, make sure you go into the phone's settings and give it permission to install apps from unknown sources—Tor will not be available in the Google Play Store, though it will be listed in the iPhone's App Store. For an Android phone, next to installing *OrWall* will force your phone's apps to use Tor exclusively. Then, installation of *OrBot* will become the gateway between your phone and the Onion Router, although you will need one last install of a browser such as *OrWeb*, to actually surf the Dark Web with your phone.

CREEPYPASTA

The tag **creepypasta** originates from the term *copypasta*, meaning text that gets copied and pasted around the internet, and sometimes in a single thread as a show of disdain and mockery. Creepypasta does not seek to mock the reader, however, its main purpose is to chill the reader into a state of fear they will never forget. Creepypasta stories rose to popularity in 2010 and moved into the public spotlight when the urban legend of *Slenderman* became national news after two girls stabbed their friend in the woods allegedly at the behest of the fictional character.

It seems natural that the misunderstood and infamous region that is the Dark Web would become the perfect catalyst for many Creepypasta stories. Creepypasta is by nature steeped in urban legends—these stories are not shared around a campfire but on a message board (and now on the website itself).

Throughout humankind's history, people have been obsessed with underground spaces. Cities beneath cities: the subterranean streets of Cappadocia, Turkey, abandoned subway tunnels of New York City, and the Parisian catacombs of death. So, has the Dark Web been a constant icon of horror and delight since its inception? These are some of the stories that have risen up from the darkness. Maybe they're real, but in all likelihood, just more urban myth being copied and pasted across the Surface Web.

A man shares his story of a friend that spoke of the darknet and became increasingly sullener and more withdrawn until the man's friend grew concerned. The friend claims he had stumbled upon a darknet site so full of horrors that it forever changed him, and claimed the site would corrupt even the best person after long enough exposure. Curious, the man asked his friend for guidance on how to get there, and after enough badgering, the friend reluctantly shared a list of sites with the caveat that he must never share the list with anyone else.

In a tarp-covered shack in a suburban patch of woods, the man's friend sat with him and sent him a text message with the site list. Then he left the shack without a word.

That night, the man installed the Tor browser and began his journey downward, starting with the first link on his friend's list. He found video footage of a local burger joint in which a mutual friend worked, and watched her exhibit strange, spooked behavior in an almost Cthulhu-esque scene where she observed invisible movement beneath the sleeves of her uniform. The man recalled she'd gone missing from town a few weeks afterward. After watching her run out of the kitchen, the man turned to the next site on the list, where he could watch live streams of so-called "red rooms". Clicking on the first stream, he saw a woman strapped to a chair and a man raising his fist to strike her. In his other hand, he held a knife. Before he could see what happened next, the hacker's friend clicked out of the video. Site after site he journeyed to the bottom of the list, unable to stay and explore the content advertised as "hacked baby monitors" and "classified federal cases". One last click and he found his screen turn pitch-black.

A speech was written just to him, using his name (which he'd never typed in) scrolled across the screen, inviting him to join a secret society. Once the speech was finished, two buttons appeared on the screen, "Join", and "Exit". When he tried to click "Exit", a pop up informed him that "exiting was not permitted". Suddenly a live feed of himself via his own webcam appeared on the screen. He tried to power down his computer but it refused to obey.

Sounds of someone breaking into his house tore him away from the demented monitor. The next thing he knew he was laying on a warehouse floor, his hands bound. Floating in and out of consciousness, he imagined a figure hovering over him, insisting he joins "We who are many in the darkness." When he woke again, he was back in his house. His friend was there, sitting next to him on the couch. "Congratulations," he said. "You passed the first test."

As fanciful as that story seems, others are far more sinister. A hobbyist hacker was lured into exploring trafficking sites by his local police department, and what he found may have cost him his life. Stumbling onto a site containing thousands of images labeled only with single names ("Alice.jpg, Jess.jpg"), he found one and clicked on it, and it seemed as if the woman was staring right at him. He began to click on other names, but the only face he saw was hers until he noticed subtle changes in her expression and in the room, she was in—what was confidence became nervousness, anxiety became outright fear, and the room was markedly darker than it was in the first image. By the time he'd clicked on the last image, he'd seen horrifying things, and the man lurking on the edges of the images who seemed to be running the show. When the police department sent someone to his home, all they found was a single file with a woman's name and several hundred lines of embedded code. The image matched the description of a woman and her parents who'd gone missing, and the hacker was never found.

HOW THE DARK WEB SAVES LIVES – LEFT IN THE COLD BY BIG PHARMA

Back to reality, there are many people with chronic illnesses who face daunting hurdles in health care systems in the US and abroad. Between the opioid crisis becoming an insurmountable roadblock in the treatment of chronic pain, to psychiatric medicine often misunderstanding and downsizing effective medication for the patients who need it the most—the worst-case scenario being someone dependent on their psychiatric drugs suddenly suffering a lapse in coverage, and having to quit their lifelines, cold turkey.

AlphaBay and Hansa (and prior, Silk Road) were shut down because of illegal drug sales, and yet these same places were havens to people failed by the system, looking for solutions to maintaining or improving their quality of life with life-saving medicine. For diabetics, the skyrocketing price of insulin has been called a criminal act in and of itself. While the epidemic sale of drugs laced with fentanyl has become an international crisis, what do the sick do when their health care system lets them down?

There are many marketplaces allegedly still in operation after the FBI takedown of the three giants. *Dream Market* and *Silk Road 3* are two of the largest. While perusing these sites means a potential client will be in very mixed company, prescription drugs can be found in the aisles right next to the illegal ones. In addition, many Surface Web online pharmacies operate Dark Web storefronts as well.

CHAPTER 5 STORIES FROM THE DARK SIDE

STORIES OF THE DARKNET

By default, the Tor browser blocks JavaScript, Java, and Flash. They can be enabled, but doing so instantly creates an identity for a Dark Web site, and for the audience viewing the video. Keep that in mind when reading the following (and disturbing) stories.

One seasoned venturer into the Dark Web claims that after a decade of merely using hidden services sites to purchase his cannabis, he decided to pry deeper, and stumbled upon a so-called "Red Room". This was no ordinary red room; however, it had a subdirectory with the tag "Coldbody". When the man clicked on that, he found a live feed with a room empty but for a stocky, dour, and bearded man standing in it, and a scrolling bar of chat to one side. Soon bodies were brought into the room, and at the encouragement of the chat users, terrible things were done to the bodies. The user left, shaken to his core.

Another story making its rounds online is one of a young man stumbling upon a classmate who'd gone missing years prior. He finds porn videos which feature her, but what chills him is her deadpan expression, and soon he realizes she is a prisoner to the ones filming the videos. He takes the story to the police but they tell him there's nothing that he can do, and best to leave it along—her family will be more comforted if they believe she's dead. Unable to do anything, he tracks down her parents and calls them. A woman answers the phone, and when he claims to know what's happening to her daughter, the woman hangs up on him.

Time passes, and his classmate's plight continues to haunt him. Then one day he gets an email from the website on which he discovered her—it's one of the site's administrators inviting him for a "special screening". Heavily conflicted, he goes to the site, frantic to find a way to help the young woman. However, what he finds once he gets there is a voice instructing her to recite a line, announcing to the audience who this scene is "for". A customer, perhaps? The young man watches as his former acquaintance is murdered, and then he realizes he recognizes the off-camera voice that coached her to speak—it was her mother's.

In another story, a site was supposedly peddling anthrax and other chemical weapons. One user talks about a red room site proven to be another hoax, called "Isis Red Room", promised to torture and kill "terrorists" for the viewers who paid top dollar. After two hours of stalling and showing plates of bacon, viewers read the announcement that the admins "lost access to the live feed, our apologies".

Many ventures into the Dark Web claim they can't shake the elaborate, disturbing images they've seen for months, or years. One account explains how a young man meandered along hidden service sites until he came to that familiarly ominous view of a black screen. For him, the only option was a blue link at the very bottom. After debating with himself as to whether or not to click it, he finally caved and entered a live stream site. Over five thousand other people were viewing the same thing, the numbers at the bottom said. A young woman in a grainy live feed capture staggered slowly across the screen, her damp, stringy hair hanging across her hollow face, makeup running in streaks. She was gaunt, underfed, her skull seemed too large for her body. Her fingertips were stained, darkened, as was a growing bruise near her mouth. A puddle lay on the ground to the right of her as she hobbled away, dragging one of her legs behind her. The young man looked closer and gasped—her mouth had been sloppily sutured closed, the black threads hanging from each corner.

Shaken, the viewer exited the room and turned off his computer. He called his girlfriend in a panic and told her he wants to file a police report, though she advised him to wait till the morning. So instead, he fell asleep.

In the morning, he retrieved his phone from the nightstand to find several outgoing calls to his girlfriend in the early hours of the morning. He also read an outgoing text—one that he himself did not send. *I can't sleep, I'm coming over.* He then read his girlfriend's reply that she'll leave the door open for him, and in a state of terror drove to her house only to find her place empty. He ran up the stairs to her bedroom and discovered her computer monitor on. Trembling, he sat at her desk and saw the same live feed he watched the night before.

Only, there were now two girls on the screen, at which point his phone vibrated, and he read the incoming text: *"You shouldn't have made that phone call."*

Yet another user claims after stumbling upon a live feed/red room site, a pop-up window asked him if he was enjoying the content. He sat, frozen to his chair, unwilling to answer until another line of text called him by his name and threatened him. He turned off his computer, but before doing so noticed he'd forgotten to tape over the webcam eye of his monitor. Several hours later, a knock at the door roused him from sleep. He stumbled down the stairs to find the front door open, and someone placed a canvas bag over his head before he was dragged out of his own house, yelling and struggling. As the streetlights shone through the rough canvas, he could make out a dark van parked in front of his house. Suddenly he could hear another man's voice shouting—it was his neighbor, taking a swing at the person holding him with a baseball bat. The man's would-be abductor stumbled away, and the van pulled out of his driveway to hurtle down the quiet residential street into the night.

A particularly enigmatic story of the Dark Web comes from San Francisco, surrounding an archaic MS-DOS game hand-crafted by some anonymous game enthusiast. The game was only distributed among several close circles of friends, and actual copies of the original game are thought to reside in landfills. Still, the game's popularity was such—and it was shared so often—that it became one of the equivalents to today's social media posts going viral. Rumors of this game lasted longer than the game itself, and this caused yet another unknown game design enthusiast to resurrect it, nearly to its last, maddening detail. The game began to circulate the text-based game enthusiast forums on various hidden service sites.

Just like before, the new game was strictly a text-based adventure. Most scenes were as minimal as this one:

You stand alone in the darkness. The light of the moon shines on the floor.

You have tools at your disposal. You have a rope. You have a treasure. A shovel leans on the wall in the corner.

You may turn East if you wish. You will find the doorway there.

Despite the game's popularity, it was also the target of great frustration. Many players had deemed it "completely unplayable and a waste of time". The only commands the game would respond to run the lines of "Take the shovel.", "Choose a door.", "Turn to the East." Many considered the game to be a superior challenge because of its simplicity—a seemingly unbreakable puzzle that only the best minds could crack. Yet most users gave up quickly and considered the game to be heavily flawed, if not simply infuriating, because from the second screen to the dozens of subsequent screens (and after the remaining three compass directions became

57

available for the player's use), only one direction would ever be the right choice, causing the player to have to backtrack through the screens and start again. Too many incorrect attempts and the game would freeze entirely and cause the player to have to reboot their computer.

Once the system was rebooted, the game seemed to take on a more demanding, concise tone. It would issue frequent statements of "*Not here*" and "*Try again*", seeming to goad and corral the player into making the right choice, though it was impossible to know what that choice was.

If the wrong tool was chosen, gameplay stopped immediately with the command "*You have made the wrong choice.*"

If a tool was selected more than once, the game would criticize, "*Be more inventive.*"

Therefore, this new reiteration of the previously popular game became a source of derision, and no one seemed to care about its outcome or purpose any longer until one player stepped up to the plate (a wealth of free time on his hands is an advantage over all). Five hours and more than thirty screens later, the user realized he'd pushed the game to crack its steely facade and offer more than just the handful of standard messages it had given him up until this moment.

The Moon smiles for you. All the roads are gone.

It seems as if a shovel could dig here. The Moon smiles for you.

Turning in the wrong direction, the game directed him to dig: *Here.* Nearly another hour later, the user managed to issue the right combination of commands, and was rewarded with coordinates:

You are successful. 41.24286_____112.4516.

After making a note of the numbers and logging off the game, the user went online to see if he could decipher the mysterious digits and realized they were the latitude and longitude of a nearby state park. Not thinking any of this was a trick, he set out to navigate the park's trails with the same tools he'd possessed in the game (in addition to a compass)—albeit lacking treasure, or possibly common sense.

The day was hot and dry, and as he climbed a steep ridge and dripped with sweat he began to wish he hadn't brought the cumbersome shovel along with him. The ridge fell away sharply and he had to circle around to regain the path toward the coordinates. The sky turned cloudy, submerging the pine woods into shadow. As he reached the other side of the ridge, he could see a thin, spidery path trailing up the other side, leading into a dark patch of forest beyond. Thunder rumbled somewhere in the distance. He wanted to finish this game before the summer rains rolled in.

The path led him to a small square of ground cleared amid a dense bed of pine needles. He began to dig. The ground was rocky and unforgiving, unlike the digitally-described terrain in the computer portion of this game. After struggling to make a dent in the plot for nearly a half hour, the shovel hit something different. Something that was not a rock.

A break in the clouds above caused a beam of sunlight to lance through the stately pines, and it shined on a dusty, blond lock of hair, unearthed by his shovel. He had found a human head, which had once been attached to the body of a little girl, but was now in advanced stages of decomposition.

Hurrying out of the park, he went directly to the local police station. The remains were identified and belonged to a little girl who had gone missing two years prior. The FBI joined the case in an effort to track down the programmer of the mysterious *Moon* game, but because the file had been swapped and traded anonymously so many times, it proved impossible to put an actual name to the crime. Archaic technology collectors and crime enthusiasts have offered six-figure rewards for an original copy of the game. The user was hailed to be a hero, though the body of the girl was never recovered.

In a less nightmare-inducing example, *Redditors* (people who frequent the message boards of the website Reddit) claimed to have found a Dark Website selling military equipment and weapons, such as fully automatic grenade launchers, but explaining how one can shoot many things from a grenade launcher—the specific ammo for it is, however, quite illegal to purchase by a civilian.

Another user talks about the infamous "Eight Levels of the Internet", the deepest layer being the so-called *"Mariana's Web"*. After searching for this layer, the user finds a window that asks, *"What do you seek?"* He types in *"enlightenment"*, and nothing happens. He pauses to give the matter some thought, and types in *"what seeks me"*, and a link appears. Following this link, he discovers a grainy live feed of soldiers in tactical gear, sweeping through the empty rooms of a derelict house until they kick in one last door to find a strange, scale-covered, humanoid creature gnawing on what looks like a human limb. Closing that link, he finds a list of undecipherable links waiting for him, and he follows them down to discover a directory of documents covering a staggering array of subjects, including human experimentation trials, alternate realities, a super-bomb hundreds of thousands of times stronger than the one dropped on Hiroshima called *"the world-ending bomb"*. The most frightening part of this list of links was, according to the viewer, no matter how far they scrolled down (and he tried for hours), the list never ended.

BACK TO REALITY

Remember when we talked about Tor blocking scripts from running? Yeah, about that.

Tor automatically blocks the programming languages that make it possible to stream live video; it allows these languages to run and will expose your identity and location to the world, hence defeating the purpose of using Tor. In addition, running live video puts a mighty strain on the network, affecting other people's use of it, placing the burden most of the volunteers running nodes. The vulnerability of plug-ins like Flash has been stated again and again by its own developers, and anyone choosing to run disturbing, illegal live stream of violent activity by using software that would act as an open window in a secure house would have to have their head examined. Furthermore, for you as the viewer, Flash and QuickTime will not work for you in Tor, so in order for you to even watch a video, you'll need to use an HTML-5 player. YouTube now uses HTML-5 after running a trial version years ago, but your YouTube account is still connected to your Google/Gmail identity, if you have one, so use carefully. Even though your IP address may be undecipherable while using Tor, your activity and behavior may become a tell to anyone watching you.

It's also possible to watch MP4 files in Tor, but in order to do so you must first enable the following lines in "*about:config*":

media.windows-media-foundation.enabled
media.directshow.enabled

Doing this will make you vulnerable to security issues, however, open to an attack should someone desire to target you.

Back to the original topic, the odds of you ever finding a real "*red room*" or torture-for-pay site are slim to none. In addition, content on Tor is typically painfully slow to load. So, what you will find are sites promising such things in exchange for your Bitcoins. View and pay at your own risk.

BACK TO UNREALITY

In addition to creepy stories of a fly on the wall red rooms and salacious chat feeds, there are the innumerable accountings of murder-for-hire websites, promising anything from image dumps of your ex invulnerable and embarrassing positions to the assassination of your boss from the job that just gave you the pink slip. "*I Will Neutralize*" is one such site, the "*Hitman Network*" (which contains a clause that they will not be contracted to target children under 16, or political figures), and "*Unfriendly Solution*" which seems to be run by someone thoroughly proud of their curmudgeonly, sadistic nature, promising to do "anything" to your target if the price is right.

One of the most famous of these sites is *Besa Mafia*, a site that also enjoys harassing any journalists who seek to report on it. The popular opinion, however, is that despite its formidable appearance and loud posturing, Besa Mafia, is—like most every other hitman-for-hire site—a scam, only after your Bitcoins with no intention of offering services. A recent data dump by activists hacking into Besa Mafia revealed elaborate messages between admins and users, showing what happens after a user pays for a hit—excuses are made, the user is lead around in virtual circles, no one is killed. At the end of the day, it's just another hustle. Not only that, other messages reveal that the site turned some users over to law enforcement. No one's sure how this is happening with identities all around being obfuscated, but the world will never be short of the naive or the careless. Besa Mafia has also been caught editing Wikipedia pages of its competitors in an effort to target them for investigation, as well as planting over-the-top, overly positive reviews of themselves throughout the Surface Net in an effort to usher new business to themselves. Finally, Besa Mafia has a referral program for its customers—recommend them to a friend and you could get a discount on your next hit.

Despite the chatter that Besa Mafia is a scam, at least one party believes they are the opposite and has put out a call for activists to try and infiltrate them and take them down. Even if the site *is* fake, the fact that people will reach out to a would-be assassin to take the lives of innocents is quite disturbing, and can lead to actual murder, as was the case of 43-year-old Minnesota man who, after attempting to contract with Besa Mafia to kill his wife, decided to take matters into his own hands (which points again to Besa Mafia being a scam, but I digress). After failing to kill her via a botched, rigged car accident, he both fed her poison and shot her, then tried to pass the murder off as suicide.

CHAPTER 6 A PRACTICAL GUIDE TO EXPLORING THE DARKWEB

THE LEGALITY OF YOUR TRAVELS

We've discussed the history and origin of The Onion Router, and how it's made up of a network of volunteers, each allowing their server to create the virtual tunnel system that affords visitors to Tor their anonymity. Still, is any of this legal?

Yes, and no.

Downloading and installing Tor is perfectly legal. Before you use it, however, it's prudent to install a VPN. Below are detailed instructions that take safety and security one step further, but at the very least, always fire up a VPN **before** you go online via Tor. Your Internet Service Provider may not be spying on you 24/7, but if they choose to look at what you're doing and see that you're on Tor, they may choose to investigate, and nobody wants their Internet access compromised.

Therefore, downloading Tor is legal. Using Tor is legal—but what you use it *for* may not be. This book highly recommends against using Tor for illegal activity. Not only is it morally wrong, but it can land you in jail. That being said, we'll cover tips on how to stay safe later on in this chapter, so you don't accidentally venture somewhere you'll later regret.

WHAT YOU'LL NEED TO START SURFING THE DARK WEB

Make sure you're using the most current version of your computer's operating system, then fire up your firewalls. Next, turn on full-disk encryption:

If you're using a **Mac**, turn on and set up FileVault by going to Apple menu > *System Preferences*, then clicking on *Security and Privacy*. Click the *FileVault* tab, then click the padlock icon and enter your administrator name and password. Click *Turn On FileVault*. Make sure you choose how to unlock your disk if you ever forget your password. You can do this using your iCloud account, by storing a recovery key linked to three security questions, or by creating a local recovery key, depending on what version of MacOS you're running (the most recent one is what you should be running!). Make sure if you choose the last option, you save the recovery key someplace other than your encrypted startup disk.

If you're using a **Windows PC**, you'll have to download a third-party encryption tool such as BitLocker, AxCrypt, VeraCrypt, or CryptLocker. Log into your Microsoft Windows account, and click on the app you've installed (for this example we'll use BitLocker). Go to Start, then click on BitLocker, then click on "*Manage BitLocker*". Next, click on "*Encrypt your full disk*". An alternate route to take is by going to "*About*" in your Start menu, then clicking on "*About Your PC*". At the bottom of the "About" page of your computer, you will see "*BitLocker Settings*", however, if that option is not there it means your computer will not allow full-disk encryption. If the option is there, click on it to complete the same task as mentioned above.

For your operating system accounts, disable *auto log in* and consider changing your passwords and (do not miss this step) *strengthening* them. Then, create an additional account, other than the administrative account to use while you surf the Dark Web.

IMPORTANT: While using this surfer account, *never* visit the Surface Web pages you usually frequent, never type your name, nicknames, friends' names, or any other personal information.

Now it's time to set up your VPN. Don't use your surfer account for this, sign back into your regular account. Now create a new Gmail address using bogus information: fake name, fake birthday - everything. Use only random letters and numbers for your username. If you need to use a phone number, grab one from here to get text messages: http://receive-sms.com.

Should you use a free VPN or pay for a monthly subscription? Times are tough, and lots of folks struggle with making ends meet, so if you opt for a free VPN service, I'll be the last person to judge you. That being said, you get what you pay for. There are free VPN's that come with good recommendations from tech sites, but the question remains, how do they make their money? Maybe by selling your information, is the troublesome thought.

Here are two lists for you to choose from – free VPNs and paid VPNs.

Top Free VPNs:

TunnelBear (whose mascot looks like it escaped from the pages of The Oatmeal, which is pretty awesome). TunnelBear offers the first month free and was recently acquired by McAfee, so I'm inclined to trust it a little more than others. It supports both desktop and mobile. The **TunnelBear** premium will only set you back $4.99 a month.

WindScribe is another free VPN that has a decently-sized data cap (unlike TunnelBear free which has a data cap of 500MB per month). It's gotten additional perks as well, such as a built-in firewall, adblocker, and awesome referral program.

ProtonVPN Free has one of the simplest sign-ups, with no monthly data limits and strict no logging procedure. It does limit you to one device, however.

Finally, **Hide.me** claims to be the world's fastest VPN. The free version allows you 2GB per month of data, and no speed throttling, plus 24/7 technical support for both free and subscription users.

The best reviewed paid VPNs for 2019 are **ExpressVPN**, **IPVanish**, **NordVPN**, **Hotspot Shield**, and **CyberGhost**.

Once you've chosen your VPN, log back into your Surfer account to download and install it. Before you connect to your VPN, select an exit location other than your own country.

Now you will install a VM (or "virtual machine") called Oracle VM VirtualBox. A VM allows you to run more than one operating system at a time. This way you can run software written for one operating system on another.

At this point, you can see where we're headed, and you'll need to make a choice about which Linux OS you'd prefer to install. If you're new to Linux (or have never used it before) opt for **Ubuntu LTS**. If you're Linux-savvy, you may enjoy **Debian GNU/Linux**.

Next, you'll need to grab yourself an **ISO** (aka an ISO image). An ISO is a file that's a perfect representation of an entire CD or DVD, the contents of which are precisely duplicated. You can get the ISO for Ubuntu here: www.ubuntu.com/desktop__. Type ISO into the search bar and this will take you to a list of ISOs' available.

Once you've downloaded the proper ISO, go ahead and start VirtualBox. Click on "*New*" and name the new virtual OS. Next, allocate the RAM you want to the new system. Click on "*Create a virtual hard disk now*", and choose "*VDI (Virtual Disk Image)*". Next, choose your preference of a Dynamically allocated of Fixed size disk. Then choose your disk's size—between 15-20GB. Now it's time to use the ISO. Browse to the ISO's folder location to help VirtualBox detect the file. Once you've opened Linux, click "*Install Ubuntu*" (or the version that you downloaded if other than Ubuntu LTS). Next, select "*Erase Disk and Install Ubuntu*". This will not erase your Windows hard drive! Right now, you're using the virtual hard drive you just created. Click "*Continue*". The remaining steps are self-explanatory from with Ubuntu and soon you'll be ready to go.

Adjust the date and time in Ubuntu to match the current local time of the VPN's exit location (remember you picked one other than your own country). From within Ubuntu, open Firefox and install the Tor browser from www.torproject.org. Once you've unzipped it, run the file *Browser/start-tor-browser*, then click "Connect". In the top-left corner, click on the onion button and select "*Security Settings*". Set your level of security to "*High*".

TIPS AND ADVICE FROM SEASONED TRAVELERS

A word of advice: using a VPN and a search engine such as **DuckDuckGo**, is prudent even if you're not using Tor. Tor is slow-going because of the extra paths data has to travel to remain encrypted. However, when you're on the Surface Web you're under the watchful eye of the King of data collection, namely Google. Google has all of your emails, text messages (if you use Android, which Google now owns), search terms, and even if you don't use Google products, their trackers can be found on millions of websites. Also, if you use Google Home, oh boy. Every live command you've given has been stored in recordings. It's worth trying to reduce your Google footprint, adventures into Dark Web aside.

Another important tool to consider adding to your kit: **Tails**. Developed by the Tor Project, Tails is a live, pre-configured Linux system that will run on nearly any machine, and can be booted from a USB drive. Purchase a new 8GB or higher flash drive and install Tails on this.

Again, make sure your machine is running *the latest version* of your OS, including the latest security patches.

Before you travel into the Dark Web, back up your important files, change your passwords, (it's recommended that you use a fresh laptop but until we all find that money tree growing in the backyard, this step's purely optional).

While you're using Tor, you can click "New circuit for this site", located in the *hamburger menu* (the menu typically comprised of three horizontal bars on any website), to reroute your path to the website of your choice and further anonymize your usage and location.

It's not recommended that you use P2P (peer to peer) or torrent sites, as doing so can navigate you too close to the line between what's legal and what's illegal. Downloading torrents is considered a reckless abuse of the system Tor intended. The design of BitTorrent's clients is not secure enough to use with Tor as the clients send your IP address to other peers. Your identity can be compromised if you use BitTorrent. In addition, make sure you delete cookies you browse sites via Tor.

Should you be worried about accidentally stumbling upon an illegal *.onion* site? If you don't have its exact address, it's impossible for you to stumble upon it. Even if you use a Tor-based search engine, the resulting lists will have text descriptions, not images, so there's no risk of your accidentally seeing something you're not supposed to (or don't want to).

Finally, the pros recommend against using Tor's Browser Bundle (but do use Tor itself). A hidden web hosting service, *Freedom*

Hosting, ran on Tor and was shut down by the FBI. It's believed that the flaws in the Browser Bundle compromised Freedom Hosting's location.

TOR IS LOOKING OUT FOR YOU (IN A GOOD WAY)

Disconnect.me, a third-party browser extension, was banned from the Google Play Store five days after its release in 2014. Google cited a violation of Terms of Service. Knowing what we now know about Google, it's easy to understand why. Disconnect.me gets in the way of data trackers turning you into their product. In May of 2015, Tor announced that Disconnect had become their official default search provider on the Tor Network. Disconnect provides private web search solutions to its users.

Each time you venture into the Darknet sites, some may be up and running, others may be temporarily down, and still, others may no longer exist. Furthermore, since a site on the Tor network takes longer than a site accessed via the Surface Web, it can be hard to tell if there's a problem or not. Going to https://check.torproject.org via the onion router will check to make sure your configuration is not the problem. The most common issue is having a discrepancy in your computer's time and date. When I visited this evening, one of my favorite sites, *Anonymous Cat Facts*, wouldn't load, but *Soylent News*, *Beneath VT* (a journey into the steam tunnels of Virginia Tech), and *The Hidden Wiki* were all loading fine.

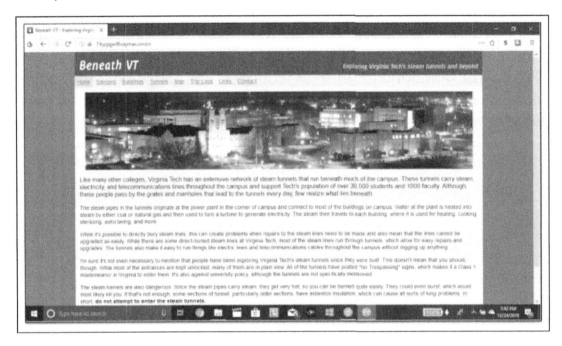

Made in the USA
Las Vegas, NV
16 April 2024

88760295R00050